C000147919

Praise

"A riveting read that finds poetry in the love and hatred hurled at news journalists."

AMY GRAFF, SFGATE NEWS EDITOR

"*Hate Mail* is a thoughtful and creative reimagining of the ugly critiques that all journalists receive while on the job. Michelle Robertson has given new life to these painful words, transforming them into something else entirely more beautiful."

JESSICA CHRISTIAN, AWARDWINNING PHOTOJOURNALIST

"Michelle Roberston is one of the few journalists I have encountered over the years who is not only a dogged reporter but also a talented writer. Her stories brilliantly span the chasm between reporting the news and spinning fascinating tales. In addition, Robertson is an interminable optimist, one who can take any situation and find an enlightened position from which to process it. These brilliant poems exhibit perseverance—a resilience that we can all learn from."

JUDY WALGREN, PULITZER PRIZE-WINNER AND ASSOCIATE DIRECTOR, MICHIGAN STATE UNIVERSITY SCHOOL OF JOURNALISM

About the Author

Michelle Robertson is a journalist based in San Francisco.
Hate Mail: Thank You for Reading is her first book.
You can read her writing at *michelle-robertson.com*

Michelle Robertson,
Hate Mail, Thank you for reading... |

Letters in Verse

A catalogue record for this book is available from the National Library of Australia

To Grandma Betty, who taught me to always talk back

Introduction

The poems in this collection represent conversations, in a sense. These conversations occurred not in person or over email, but in my mind, between myself and those who had written to me over the two-and-a-half years I worked as a reporter at the second-largest newspaper site in California. In that time, I received hundreds of emails and letters from across the US. Some of these letters were thoughtful, kind, patient. Most of them were written in anger—at my writing, at the subject matter, at me.

Receiving hate mail is a rite of passage in the newspaper business. A letter means someone has read what you wrote, cares enough to take the time to talk back to the story. What is sometimes forgotten, and what these letters signify, is that behind the story—behind the email address—sits a human being. I read every letter I received. I did not always reply, especially to some of the more vicious emails, many of which are included in this book. Replying, I found, sometimes opened up a floodgate of further hatred and vitriol. The back and forth, in many cases, was one-sided and unfruitful. Then again, I often just didn't have the time.

Hate mail is naturally poetic, even without the intervention of the poet. The letters I received were often lyrical in their emotional tenor. The words used were selected, perhaps haphazardly (typos and spelling errors have, in most instances, been preserved), but in the interest of conjuring anger, displeasure, joy, or recognition. I don't think all of these letters were written in the interest of receiving a response. Rather, I believe many felt compelled to write to me due to an overflowing of emotion incited by my stories. These poems represent a release of energy, stored up over weeks, months, perhaps years.

The poems in this collection are a way of talking back to the original authors, of recognizing the weight of their words and the poetry concealed within them. I conceived of the project as a sculptor would: the emails are stone, awaiting attention and the transformation that accompanies it.

These poems are conversations but also translations. I hoped to sculpt these oft-quickly written emails into something else: an object for public contemplation. What do these letters have to say about the public perception of journalists? Of female journalists? Of the state of a bipartisan country? Through translation, the answers come into the light.

I have edited the poems in this collection only minimally, inserting line and stanza breaks, capitalizations and light punctuation where necessary. They are the culmination of texts talking back to texts talking back to texts.

John Coward

Jesus fucking christ. Are you a journalist?
James Demore — "memo claiming men

Are biologically better-suited
To coding than woman."

He never said that. Get out of your
Safe space and look at the facts.

Millennials are insane. Get a clue
Babe. This public lie is shameful.

Do your parents know your spouting bullshit???

Gregory

Now, you sound like someone
Looking for a fight.

Message from Jim

Michelle Robertson ...

Is nothing but a coward
And a stupid bitch behind a pen.

Adios liberal piece of shit!

Gordon

Why now

OMG

I have blue eyes.
Does this mean
I am a mutant?

Edwin

I feel the need to defend the actions
Of these bears

As it was humans feeding them
That led to nearly being killed
As a punishment by humans.

Also, as a parent, what would you do
To feed your children?

Meet Our Lord Sandwich

Enjoyed your pet influencer feature!
Meet our Lord Sandwich.

Instadogs

Those dogs are
Corporate sellouts.

Poetic Justice, Part Two

Take all the studies and shove 'em.
It's all about greed, pure and simple.

Just greed.

Greed. Greed. Greed.
Greed. Greed Greed. Greed ...

My advice

Stay away from blue states and cities
Where fecal street maps are part of
The welcome package for visitors.

K

Psycho Big mouth Waters
Nothing but ball less coward

Poetic Justice

I don't know if you write your headlines
Or if some other semi-literate does it.

"Die-Off" is correct ONLY when used as a noun.
As a verb IT IS STILL TWO SEPARATE WORDS—

JUST TWO SEPARATE WORDS LIKE ANY
OTHER TWO SEPARATE WORDS!!!!!!!!

What is the matter with you Ignoramuses?

R

Big mouth coward democrats
Turn and run—no plan, no
Agenda for America

Flinstone house

I pulled up when I read your description
Of that stretch of I-280 as "banal".
It's actually one of the most
Beautiful expressways in the world.

Guess you haven't seen the fog cling to the surface
Of the reservoir, filter the sunlight,
Curl around the roadway and disappear.

Kavanaugh

Kavanaugh was passionate and articulate,
And offered clear, concise evidence.

Ford gave us nothing but emotions.

Yes, we can call out liars
who happen to be women.

Gender equality, right?

BTW, cherry-picking the rants of Leftist
Internet trolls does not constitute news.

Thanks for reading.

Aubrey

Shut up with your stupid troll
article. Wish you got hit
by a car while you we're
at it. You get your stupid
lanes in the city already
so shut the fuck up.

Noodle

So, you gave up using the noodle
Because it slowed YOU down.
Oh, ok.

Unbelievably selfish

Your noodle trick. OMG.
Your antic has now proven
Beyond a doubt: bike riders

Are selfish, selfish, selfish
Rude people. Unbelievable.

Me me me me me
Me me me me me me

May you all be banned from the roads,
Trails, everywhere forever.

A PhD in English Literature

Really? Put that in bad decisions
By San Francisco exiles file.

Get a marketable skill.
And I don't mean Anthropology :).

Reporter Attacked

Surprised it doesn't happen more often,
especially in the video media.

- Stick a mic in someone's face after violence
  or disaster and ask "How do you feel?"
- Get the facts wrong.
- Disrespect private property.
- Spin the facts to the reporter's employer's bias
  (as in Jeff Bezos and *The Washington Post*)
- Overuse of adjectives, breathless delivery
  word/phrase emphasis to sensationalize
  the piece, as appears to be the case
  in your article.

Just saying ... There is a difference
between journalism professionals
who claim to "report" for media outlets.

Roll of Shame

Do you think we can sell
A MILLION rolls of toilet paper
With Kaepernick's photo?

NBA Didn't Start Flat Earth

"Here's hoping this flat-Earth trend
Doesn't spread beyond the NBA."

Here's hoping that such disingenuous
Comments are not rewarded.

Kenyon

Why does your article read
As if she was somehow entitled
To live where she grew up

And was robbed by unseen forces
That conspired against her?

What part did her own decisions
Play in her narrative?
What part did you, the author have in buying
Into the narrative?

Were you thinking critically,
Or emotionally/empathetically?

John

I don't think you meant to use the word
"Urbanity" to describe urban sprawl.

Urbanity means:
> n. Refinement and elegance of manner;
>   Polished courtesy
> n. Courtesies; civilities.

I am trying to be "urbane" here, not rude.

Joe Shmo

SELF RIGHTEOUS SELFISH ASS
NO WONDER YOUR RAG
LOSES $1 MILLION A DAY

In the Comment Section

E: They could use more attractive shelf talkers.

S: By your picture, I wouldn't be calling anybody unattractive ever!!!

E: A shelf talker is the written description of the product on the shelf above it.
I wasn't referring to the woman who narrating the video.
I also won't add a insult of my own about you and your lack of knowledge about this.

M: The plastic woman goes quickly on the defensive. Imagine that!

Article you wrote

You wrote an article, I'm curious though,
Did you see the security footage?

I'll give you the dog is small, but it's unleashed
and appears to attack him first...

Dead whales and commercial fishing

If whales cannot find food, are commercial
Fishermen catching fewer fish?

Do restaurants at Fisherman's Wharf
Have a shortage of fresh fish?

dredging

Not even a mention on the ignorance
Driven ban on suction drudging?

Are you too lazy to research,
Too ignorant to know,
Or so partisan like your handlers

That you are happy to obfuscate
Because you just don't give a shit
About people and their lively hoods.

Dumb cunt.

O Kap Mein Kap

The road not taken reminds me
The courage of taking on the unknown.

Life is what we make out to be.
No fear.

And best wishes in your pursuit
Of life and letters.

Paul

Michelle,
You should visit Wilmington, NC.
Paul

Response to Article

How you know you're done with San Francisco
Whoever wrote this isn't an adult or a local ...
Go home now!

Good luck in SoCal

Thanks for all your writings.
You are excellent.

Home will be where you make it
no matter the color of the grass.

Orange County is like San Francisco

It has nice weather,
Insane real estate prices,
Happiness destroying traffic,
And a bounty of homeless people.

Article about Bakersfield

I'm focused, is your nose
So high up in the air

Because you are an entitled snob
Or because you can't stand
The poop smell Everytime
You walk down the street?

Maybe you should leave your bubble
Sometime and venture out to visit
Someplace that doesn't require
A tetanus shot just to leave your home.

Southern boyfriend

He didn't ask about rats
The size of cats
On Market Street?

And his car hasn't
Been broken into?
Hmmm.

Story idea

It's not a right now story Michelle,
People are still being killed and that's
Your bottom line is to deliver that.

A long researched in-depth story that delivers
And shows the depth of the research.

Richard

"In the surveillance video,
He wears a black Jordan brand hat,
A black T-shirt featuring
Marilyn Monroe, and carries
Two black backpacks in each hand."

Is wearing is carrying
A black backpack in each hand

(Unless you mean a total of 4 backpacks)

What ...

Fake news at its very best.
Anyone that believes

This article is reality
Is either really HIGH

Or just plane stupid.
And stupid is harder to fix.

What Change?

While the idea is good,
The execution so far
Is lacking substance.

So you fluffed one.
Let's try harder
On the next story.

Your Article

Writing is improved when you avoid
Repeating pronouns

"they, themselves"
"me, myself"

and the title
"I'm leaving...myself"—
"I'm, leaving" should suffice.

Good luck on your next quest!

Love and Security

Go together, right? After doing some
Grocery shopping at Church St Safeway,

I sat down with a cup of coffee
And a muffin. The whole time I took
That break, the security guard at her post
By the door lip-locked with her boyfriend
And just embraced each other like he
Had just returned from a foreign war.

I was very intrigued by this tempestuous
Activity. If you hurry you might catch a sight.

Berkeley Bowl

Omg thanks for the pic in the article.
I thought it was a bowling alley ...

Ben

Robertson writes that this guy is on enough
Romance novels "to fill a two-year calendar
Of washboard abs and female fantasy."

And I want to ask my gay and lesbian friends:
What are YOUR fantasies about queer erasure?

Debra

I, and everyone on 18th street
(From Douglass to the end) are THRILLED
By the new lights on our street.

No more do we have to worry
About people lurking in the dark
Ready to pounce and rob us,
Or worse yet selling drugs.

SAUCED

It is not
A Joint.

Response to Article

[REDACTED] should be real news and not tabloid /
Real estate shit geared to the hipster /
Techie cultures which have destroyed the soul

Of our once enchanting City.

Your article was elitest and disgusting.
NOT CLEVER OR FUNNY. Please move back
From where you came from.

Feminist Extremist

Are you also a Feminist Extremist
Or the so called 'Women's Rights Activist,'
The likes of Ms. Michele Dauber?

About your report on September 14, 2017:
'Brock Turner now the textbook
Definition of 'rape' in criminal justice book,'

___Ms. Robertson, don't be radical,
Don't be an agitator,
And don't be Naive!
You are gambling the credibility and integrity
Of your company, [REDACTED],
in writing such a report;

Chris B

This dude is not a star He's crowdfunding
To pay for a deductible and security guards.

He can pretend to be as gangster
As you think he is, but again ...
Crowdfunding security guards

Two more things,
1.) It wasn't a $90K camera,
     let's be honest
2.) You might be retarded
     to even call this article journalism.

I'm sure your parents are secretly
Disappointed in you. Clown shoes

David

I cannot [sic] say no to
Convenience and affordability.
I CHOOSE not to say no ...
FTFY.

Ann

I'm excited to see the film
Of the narwhales—

But it won't come up on the screen.
Can you help?

Good for you

I can feel your tension though.
Most noodles are hollow
And seem like a good place
To tape a magic marker.

Cyclist and Mom

As a cyclist and mom,
Please tighten your helmet straps!

It's not going to do you much good
If it goes flying off your head
Before it can do
What it's meant to do!

Dear Michelle

All the valid points in your article disappear
When seeing you proceed to walk down a sidewalk
With the it hanging off the side
Forcing pedestrians to avoid you.

Your actions show lack of situational awareness
And ruin your story.

How can you possibly think
This is OK?

Scandal

Q. Why do jocks choose USC over UCLA?
A. Easier to spell.

Tim

HOW MANY TIMES ARE YOU GOING TO PRINT
THIS FUCKING ARTICLE ABOUT FOLKS
WHO MOVED NW. WHO THE FUCK CARES

Response to Article

The photos that have been selected
to pair with the captions are offensive

and I suggest you change the accompanying
photos or take down this article.

Dear Michelle,

With due respect, this exact article
Ran on [REDACTED] not two months ago.

Are you a bit embarrassed to be associated
With such a witless enterprise.

Why not use your skills in a more
Dignified manner.

Shutter

You mean to say shudders
Instead of shutters.

Low literacy levels contribute
To making America stupid.

Acknowledgements

This book would not have been possible, on principle, without my readers. I'm grateful to them and their many emails. Thank you to my parents, Jan and Ted, for teaching me that my voice mattered. To everyone who read early drafts, provided feedback and encouraged me this book was worth writing—you made *Hate Mail* what it is and for that, I'm eternally grateful. A special thanks to Amie and Jessica and everyone at Vine Leaves Press for bringing this book to the world. To Orion, my world and biggest fan. And lastly, to all female journalists who do what they do every day. I'm in awe of you all.

Vine Leaves Press

Enjoyed this book?
Go to *vineleavespress.com* to find more.

9 780645 436503